D1378501

ROBOTS AND ROBOTICS

Film and Fiction Robots

Tony Hyland

Smart Apple Media

Smart Apple Media
2140 Howard Drive West
North Mankato, Minnesota 56003

First published in 2007 by
MACMILLAN EDUCATION AUSTRALIA PTY LTD
627 Chapel Street, South Yarra, Australia 3141

Visit our Web site at www.macmillan.com.au or go directly to www.macmillanlibrary.com.au

Associated companies and representatives throughout the world.

Library of Congress Cataloging-in-Publication Data

Hyland, Tony.
    Film and fiction robots / by Tony Hyland.
    p. cm. — (Robots and robotics)
    Includes index.
    ISBN 978-1-59920-120-7
    1. Robots—Juvenile literature. 2. Stage props—Juvenile literature. 3. Cinematography—Special
effects—Juvenile literature. 4. Science fiction films—Juvenile literature. 5. Motion pictures—Plots,
themes, etc.—Juvenile literature. 6. Science fiction—Juvenile literature. I. Title.

    TJ211.2.H536 2007
    629.8'92—dc22

                                                                        2007004745

Edited by Margaret Maher
Text and cover design by Ivan Finnegan, iF Design
Page layout by Ivan Finnegan, iF Design
Photo research by Legend Images

Printed in U.S.

Acknowledgements
The author and the publisher are grateful to the following for permission to reproduce copyright material:

Front cover photograph: Still from the movie Robots courtesy Movie Store Collection Ltd.

Photos courtesy of:
© Mary Evans Picture Library/Alamy, pp. 7, 10, 11; Aquarius Collection, ©20th Century Fox, p. 5; Aquarius Collection/ ©MGM, p. 14; © BBC/ Corbis, p. 8; © Bettmann/Corbis, pp. 9, 15; © Douglas Kirkland/Corbis, p. 12; © Frank Trapper/Corbis, p. 19; © Les3photo8/Dreamstime.com, p. 6; Gustavo Caballero/Getty Images, p. 27; Front cover of I, Robot, Oxford University Press, UK, image from Getty Images/Image Bank/Joseph Grivas, p. 13; © Hasbro, pp. 4, 25; ©2006 The LEGO Group, p. 29; LUCASFILM LTD/David Owen, pp. 22, 23; Movie Store Collection Ltd, pp. 20, 21; ANI/ Movie Store Collection Ltd, p. 28; LUCASFILM/Movie Store Collection Ltd, pp. 1, 16, 17, 18; Star Trek/Movie Store Collection Ltd, p. 24; © Kin Cheung/Reuters/Picture Media, p. 26.

Background textures courtesy of Photodisc.

While every care has been taken to trace and acknowledge copyright, the publisher tenders their apologies for any accidental infringement where copyright has proved untraceable. Where the attempt has been unsuccessful, the publisher welcomes information that would redress the situation.

Contents

GLOSSARY WORDS
When a word is printed in **bold**, you can look up its meaning in the glossary on page 31.

Robots

There are more and more robots in the world. Once they were just figments of the imagination, metal creatures that clanked through old **science fiction** movies and books. Robots today are real, and you will find them in the most surprising places. Some are tiny, no bigger than a fly. Others are among the largest machines on Earth.

Robots are machines that can move and think for themselves. Most robots work in factories, doing endless, repeated tasks faster than any human. Other robots explore places that humans cannot safely reach. Some robots go to the bottom of the sea. Others go to the rocky surface of Mars.

There are also **surgical robots**, robots that carry out scientific experiments, and robots that **disarm** bombs. Today's toys often include robot technology—you can even **program** your own toy robot.

Where do robots fit into your life?

Transformers are popular toy robots.

Film and fiction robots

The real robots of this world are interesting, but not very exciting. They work away at their jobs, doing exactly as they are told. They have a low level of **artificial intelligence**.

In films and fiction, however, robots can do anything. Imaginary robots can be huge metal monsters or tiny flying gizmos. They can look and act almost human, or be scary and alien. Above all, they can be intelligent and have minds of their own.

We see imaginary robots on TV or at the movies. We read about them in books and comics, or battle them in computer games. Even before there was such a word as "robot," people imagined what it would be like if a statue could come to life.

With today's powerful **computer graphics**, movie **animators** can make robot armies battle on-screen. They can show robots far more advanced than any robot in our world today.

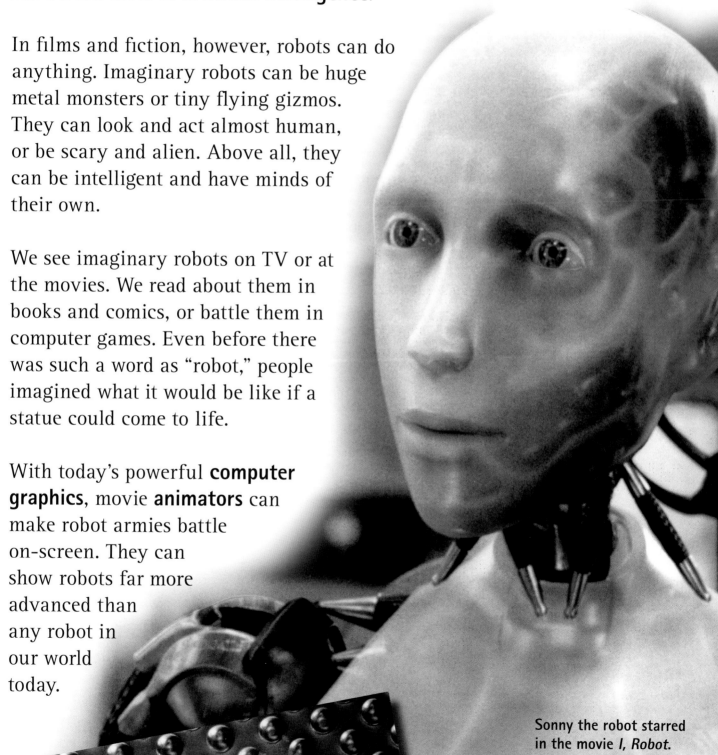

Sonny the robot starred in the movie *I, Robot.*

5

The first robots

The idea of bringing a mechanical creature to life has fascinated people for thousands of years. The ancient Greeks tell the story of the sculptor Pygmalion. He made a statue so beautiful that he fell in love with it. The goddess Aphrodite brought it to life.

Mechanical figures

Long ago, Greek and Roman scientists worked out how to make mechanical figures. One famous Greek scientist made a complete mechanical puppet theater. It worked with a complicated set of **gears**, ropes, and **pulleys**. He even made mechanical birds that could flap their wings and whistle.

ROBOFACT

THE LEGEND OF THE GOLEM

An ancient Jewish tale tells of the wise **rabbi** Judah Loew. He made a huge clay **golem** to protect the Jewish people of Prague. But the golem was big and frightening. Rabbi Loew took away its magic, for fear that it would hurt his people.

The ancient Greeks told a story about a statue that came to life.

Automatons

In the 1500s, engineers began using clockwork to make moving mechanical figures. These figures were known as automatons.

Automatons were made in the shape of animals, birds, and even people. The figures were not robots as we know them. They were clever toys that could repeat certain actions over and over. But many people thought it might be possible to make automatons so realistic that they could pass as human.

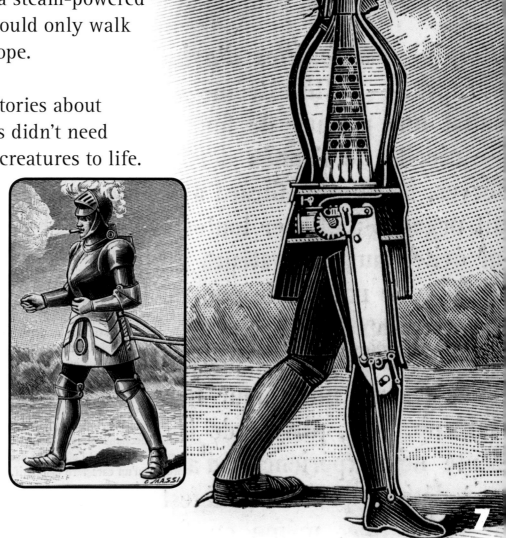

The steam-powered automaton was unable to do anything except walk in a circle.

Steam-powered automatons

When steam engines were developed in the 1800s, several engineers tried to build steam-driven automatons. One Canadian inventor built a steam-powered automaton. However, it could only walk around in a circle on a rope.

Authors began to write stories about automatons. These stories didn't need magic to bring artificial creatures to life. The writers imagined that scientists would develop new and smarter automatons—mechanical servants with a brain. In the 1900s, these new stories came to be known as science fiction.

Early film and fiction robots

During the 1920s, a stage play and a silent movie gave us the first stories of modern robots. These stories were the start of a whole new type of fiction, known as science fiction.

Rossum's Universal Robots

In 1920, Karel Capek, a Czech playwright, wrote a play called *Rossum's Universal Robots*. The word *robota* is Czech for "hard work." *Rossum's Universal Robots* was about a company that produced thousands of robots. The robots were intelligent, but had no soul and no feelings. Eventually the robots rebelled.

The play was a huge success. Soon the word "robot" was known throughout the world.

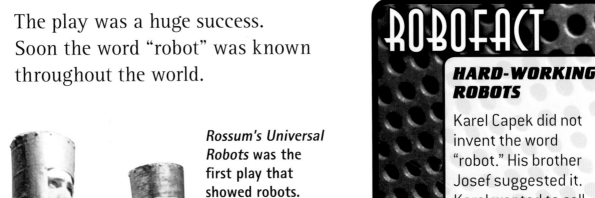

Rossum's Universal Robots was the first play that showed robots.

ROBOFACT

HARD-WORKING ROBOTS

Karel Capek did not invent the word "robot." His brother Josef suggested it. Karel wanted to call his creatures *delnas*, another Czech word that also means "hard workers." If he had, none of us would even know the word "robot"!

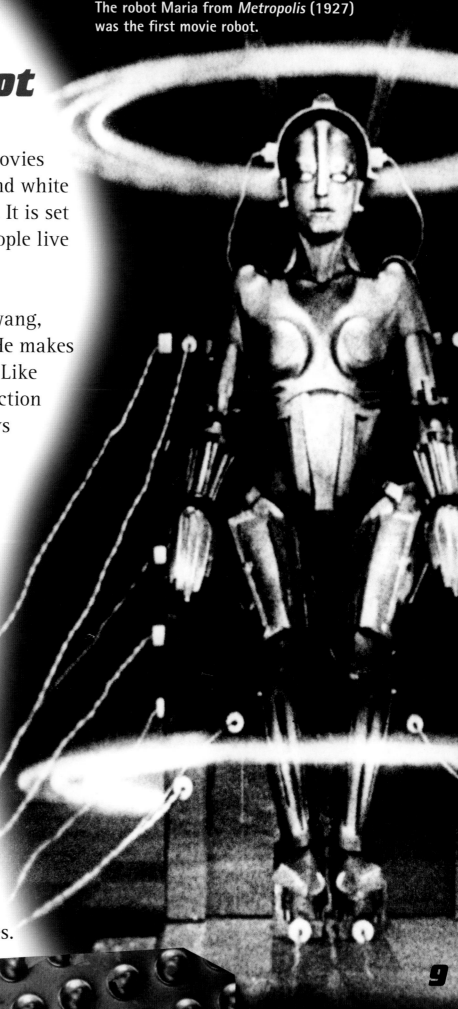

The robot Maria from *Metropolis* (1927) was the first movie robot.

The first robot movie

The first of the early robot movies was *Metropolis*. This black and white silent film was made in 1927. It is set in a distant future, where people live and work in a huge city.

In the movie a scientist, Rotwang, creates an intelligent robot. He makes it look like a human woman. Like the robots in many science fiction stories, the robot at first obeys its maker. Later, however, it ignores his wishes. It stirs up a **revolt** among the workers of Metropolis before it is eventually destroyed.

Losing control

One of the common ideas in stories about robots is that the makers lose control of their robots. This happens in both *Metropolis* and *Rossum's Universal Robots*. It also happens in many of the robot stories that came after them. People find this idea both exciting and scary—and that makes it perfect for entertaining stories.

Science fiction magazines

During the 1920s and 1930s, people wanted to read stories about robots, space travel, and aliens. Dozens of new science fiction magazines started up, each one with many new stories.

Science fiction magazines, such as *Astounding Science Fiction* and *Amazing Stories,* ran for many years. Most of the stories in them were exciting adventures. There were stories about aliens attacking Earth and robot armies going into battle.

Robots in most of these stories were terrifying machines. Often they were controlled by evil masters. Many robots in these stories were built by scientists. However, the robots turned against their creators and destroyed them.

Astounding Science Fiction introduced many new stories about robots.

ROBOFACT

SCIENCE FICTION WRITERS

Some of the most famous science fiction authors first wrote stories for science fiction magazines. Isaac Asimov, Robert Heinlein, and Arthur C. Clarke all wrote for magazines during the 1930s. Their stories and ideas are still used in modern movies and TV shows.

The spread of science fiction magazines

Science fiction magazines were printed on cheap paper, and the stories were often poorly written. Still, millions of readers enjoyed them. Over and over, writers produced similar stories, with heroes fighting evil aliens and fearsome robots.

Good and evil robots

Not all the robots in science fiction stories were evil. Some were good servants. Some were tireless workers who could work all day and night in factories. Others were almost human, and able to fit in with human society. Robots could be or do anything that authors could imagine.

Adam Link

In the late 1930s, Eando Binder wrote a series of stories about a heroic robot called Adam Link. Adam becomes a detective, saves the world, and even travels back in time.

The first of these stories was called "I, Robot." Later, this title was used by another famous writer, Isaac Asimov, for his book of robot stories.

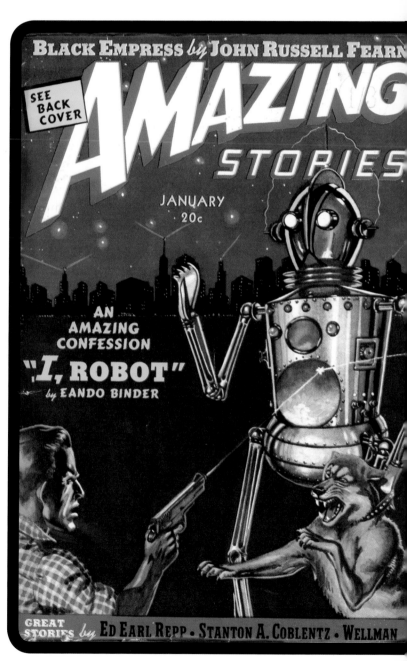

Eando Binder wrote many stories about a robot called Adam Link.

Isaac Asimov

Isaac Asimov was a famous science fiction writer. In 1940, he made up laws for the robots in his stories. These laws changed the way most robots in stories and movies behaved from then on.

Asimov wondered what society would be like if robots really existed. He thought robots should have built-in laws to stop them from hurting people. Most of the robots in science fiction stories seemed to attack humans. Asimov decided robots should not be able to do this.

Isaac Asimov wrote many robot stories, all based on his famous Laws of Robotics.

ASIMOV'S LAWS OF ROBOTICS

First Law: A robot may not injure a human being, or, through inaction, allow a human being to come to harm.

Second Law: A robot must obey orders it is given by human beings, except where such orders would **conflict** with the First Law.

Third Law: A robot must protect its own existence, as long as such protection does not conflict with the First or Second Laws.

Up Close

ROBOT
Robbie the robot

FEATURED IN
"Strange Playfellow" in *I, Robot*

JOB
Personal servant

MAKER
U.S. Robots

SKILLS
Cleaning the house and looking after children

SIZE
69 inches (175 cm) tall

Robbie is one of the first robots to follow Asimov's laws. He first appeared in the story "Strange Playfellow." This is one of many short stories in Asimov's book *I, Robot*. He is a **humanoid** robot with two legs.

Robbie's main job is to look after Gloria, the daughter of the family Robbie works for. But Gloria's mother doesn't trust robots. She demands that Robbie be sent back to the factory.

Later, Robbie proves that he can be trusted, when he rescues Gloria from an accident at the robot factory.

Asimov's stories feature Dr. Susan Calvin, a **psychologist**. Most psychologists are experts in understanding the human mind. Susan is an expert in the workings of robot minds.

Robot movies

Robots were featured in some early science fiction movies. They were nearly always shown as evil creations, ready to do the will of their master.

During the 1930s and 1940s, movie studios made many cheap science fiction movies. They were popular children's entertainment.

Classic robot movies

Two classic movies of the 1950s featured robots that are still recognized today. Gort was the giant robot of *The Day the Earth Stood Still*. He protected his master Klaatu, who had come to Earth to spread a message of peace. Like the book *I, Robot*, *Forbidden Planet* features a robot called Robbie. He is the perfect servant. Though he is a huge metal creature, he prepares meals, offers drinks, and even tells jokes.

ROBOFACT

ROBBIE THE ROBOT

In *Forbidden Planet*, Robbie the Robot was played by an actor inside a robot suit. The original Robbie suit was later used in other movies and TV shows.

Robbie the Robot appeared in the classic movie *Forbidden Planet*.

Early science fiction movies

Like the science fiction magazines, most of the science fiction movies of the 1950s and 1960s were cheap and poorly made. Some of the better known movies are *Tobor the Great* (1954), *The Invisible Boy* (1957), and *King Kong Escapes* (1967).

Tobor the Great

Tobor is a robot that has been made to pilot a spaceship to Mars. It can be controlled by its master's thoughts. When the inventor and his grandson are kidnapped by spies, Tobor comes to the rescue.

The Invisible Boy

The Robbie suit from *Forbidden Planet* was used again for this movie. Robbie teams up with a boy to fight a powerful computer that threatens to take control of Earth.

King Kong Escapes

This movie actually has two King Kongs—the "real" one, and a huge robot King Kong, called MechaKong. The two Kongs battle each other on top of the Tokyo Tower in Japan.

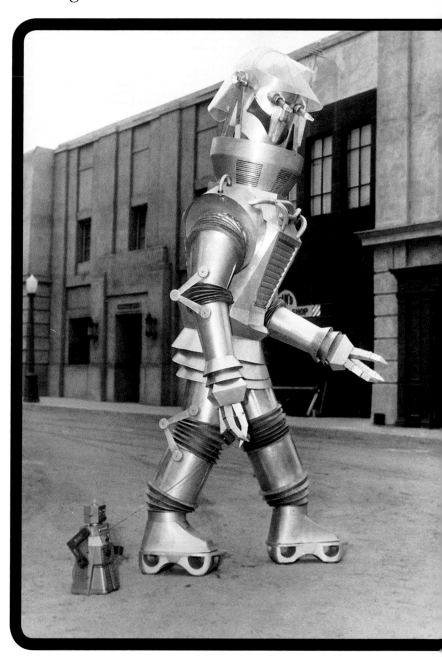

Tobor, the giant robot, rescued his master from kidnappers.

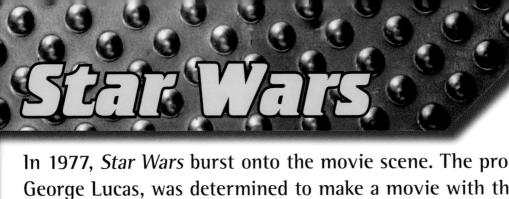

In 1977, *Star Wars* burst onto the movie scene. The producer, George Lucas, was determined to make a movie with the best **special effects** possible. Audiences could see robots that looked realistic and had personality.

Star Wars robots

The two main robots of all six *Star Wars* movies are R2-D2 and C-3PO. They are always around to help the human characters.

R2-D2 is short and friendly. It rolls along on three wheels, chirping and whistling in its own language. It can work as a spaceship mechanic or computer expert.

C-3PO is polite and helpful, but he is always anxious that things will go wrong. He speaks six million languages, which makes him very useful.

C–3PO and R2–D2 appeared in all six *Star Wars* movies.

ROBOFACT

WHY ARE THEY CALLED DROIDS?

In *Star Wars* movies, robots are called droids. The word is short for android, which means "like a human." The word android is often used for robots that look human, rather than machines like R2-D2.

Meet the droids

The *Star Wars* movies introduced dozens of robots. Some, like R2-D2 and C-3PO, were helpers. Others were fierce and powerful fighters.

The helper droids

The surgical droid 2-1B is a humanoid robot with a skull-like head. It has many surgical instruments attached to it.

MSE-6 droids are small, box-shaped messengers. They roll around the passageways of factories and the Death Star, the secret battle station of the Galactic Empire.

The fighter droids

Super battle droids are humanoid robots covered in strong armor. They charge into battle, firing their arm blasters—**laser** weapons built into their arms.

Droidekas are large, insect-like robots, armed with blasters. They can fold themselves up into a disk shape, rolling swiftly into battle.

In the original three *Star Wars* movies, the robots were mainly models, or humans inside costumes. For the later movies, the producers used computer graphics to make hundreds of robots appear on the screen.

The armies of super battle droids were made entirely by computer graphics.

Creating realistic robots

How do movie makers create a realistic robot? Let's see some of the robot special effects behind the movies.

The actor in the robot suit

British actor Anthony Daniels plays the part of C-3PO. In the first three movies, he wore a robot suit. He had to act his parts without speaking, as his voice could not be heard through the mask. The voice parts were recorded later.

The person behind C-3PO

In *Star Wars Episode 1: The Phantom Menace*, C-3PO was built as a full-size puppet. A person controlled the puppet while standing behind it. Later, computer special effects people removed all signs of the person.

ROBOFACT

STAR WARS WITHOUT DROIDS

When *Star Wars* was first written, there were no droids in the story. The writer used two bumbling humans to add humor to the story. Luckily for us, these characters were changed to R2-D2 and C-3PO.

Anthony Daniels, who plays C-3PO, removes part of his costume.

Up Close

ROBOT
R2-D2 ("Artoo" to his friends)

JOB
Astromech droid

MAKER
Industrial Automaton

SKILLS
starship mechanic and
computer interface specialist

SIZE
38 inches (97 cm) tall

R2-D2 is a small robot, just over 3 feet (97 cm) tall. He is an interesting and appealing character. His head turns, his lights flash, and he whistles and makes other odd noises.

Most of R2-D2's personality comes from the actor who controls him. Sitting inside the suit, Kenny Baker has control over lights and switches that make all of Artoo's movements.

Several **radio-controlled models** were also used in the movie. When the robot is rolling across open areas, it is usually the radio-controlled model.

In the first three *Star Wars* movies, the radio-controlled models often stopped working. This caused problems for the **film crew**. In the later movies, the models worked much better. Kenny had less to do, because the models were able to do some of his work.

Modern robot movies

Many modern science fiction movies feature robots. Movie producers realized that robots did not need to be awkward metal monsters, but could appear almost human.

Terminator and Robocop

The three *Terminator* movies (1984–2003) starred Arnold Schwarzenegger as an unstoppable android. He appears to be human, but when he is damaged, we see robot parts inside his body. The android in *RoboCop* (1987) is made from an injured human policeman. The policeman's uninjured brain and nerves power a robot body.

Fitting in with human society

Robot movies are often about an android trying to fit in with human society. In *Bicentennial Man* (1999), a robot spends 200 years trying to become completely human. In *AI: Artificial Intelligence* (2001), David the robot boy looks for someone who will love him.

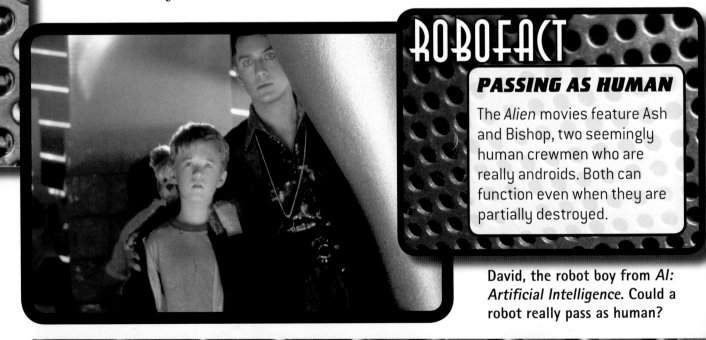

ROBOFACT

PASSING AS HUMAN

The *Alien* movies feature Ash and Bishop, two seemingly human crewmen who are really androids. Both can function even when they are partially destroyed.

David, the robot boy from *AI: Artificial Intelligence*. Could a robot really pass as human?

Machines with personality

Sometimes, a movie robot really does look like a robot. Movie producers saw that robots could look like machines but still show human personality.

※ Johnny Five, from *Short Circuit* (1986), is a robot loaded with deadly weapons. But when he is struck by lightning, he suddenly becomes intelligent and aware—and cute.

※ *The Iron Giant* (1999) is a huge, gentle iron robot. He is in danger from government forces who want to destroy him.

※ *I, Robot* (2004) is loosely based on Isaac Asimov's stories. It is set in a future when robots are common. The robots are unable to harm humans, because they have Asimov's Laws of Robotics built in, but one robot is accused of murder.

※ The cartoon movie *Robots* (2005) is the story of Rodney Copperbottom. Rodney is a young robot who lives in a world where all the inhabitants are robots.

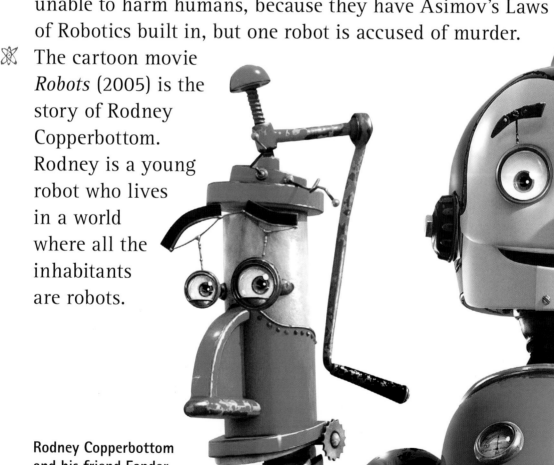

Rodney Copperbottom and his friend Fender starred in *Robots* (2005).

Designing robots

Movie studios can create amazing robots using computer generated images (CGI). How do they produce scenes with dozens of realistic, detailed robots?

1. Preparing the design

First, illustrators sketch designs for the different types of robots. They draw each figure from many different angles and in different poses. The **director** chooses the figures that seem best for the movie.

An illustrator draws the first designs for a robot.

2. Digitizing the figures

The completed sketches of the figures are then digitized, or copied into the computer. The animators build up a three-dimensional image of the robot from the sketches. They draw **wire-frame outlines** of the figures on-screen. Then, the figures are covered with realistic, computer-drawn skin.

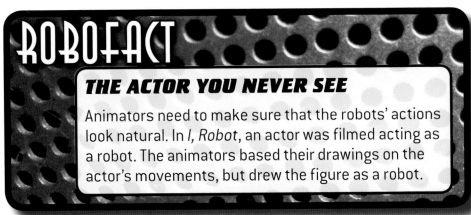

ROBOFACT

THE ACTOR YOU NEVER SEE

Animators need to make sure that the robots' actions look natural. In *I, Robot*, an actor was filmed acting as a robot. The animators based their drawings on the actor's movements, but drew the figure as a robot.

3. Animating the figures

The head, arms, and legs of each robot are animated separately, so that all of the parts look as if they move naturally. It takes hundreds of hours to complete the movements for each figure. The robot figures can then be made to walk, run, talk, or fight.

An animator makes each section of the drawing move.

4. Bringing the figures to life

Once the figures move smoothly, the movements have to be matched to the action of the movie. Animators produce an image of one robot. They then place the same image over and over in different places on the screen. One figure suddenly turns into an army.

Each image can be made to work separately from the others. This means the screen can show many similar robots doing different actions. In a battle scene, some could be attacking, while others will be retreating. Yet all are made from the one original image.

Robots on TV

Many TV shows have featured robots. Both live action and cartoon shows have used robots as main characters.

TV shows are made quickly. They do not have the time or the budgets that movies do. The easiest way to show robots on TV shows is to use human actors or cartoon characters.

Some robots from popular TV shows are:

* Rosie the maid from *The Jetsons*
* Astro Boy, a powerful robot with the appearance of a young boy, from *Astro Boy*
* Haro, from *Mobile Suit Gundam*
* Optimus Prime from *Transformers*
* "Jenny" XJ-9 Wakeman from *My Life as a Teenage Robot*
* Commander Data from *Star Trek: The Next Generation*
* Bender from *Futurama*

ROBOFACT

THE OLDEST ROBOT TV STAR

The original *Astro Boy* comics started in Japan in 1952. In the 1960s, the first *Astro Boy* cartoons appeared on television. More episodes were made in the 1980s, and yet another series was made in 2003.

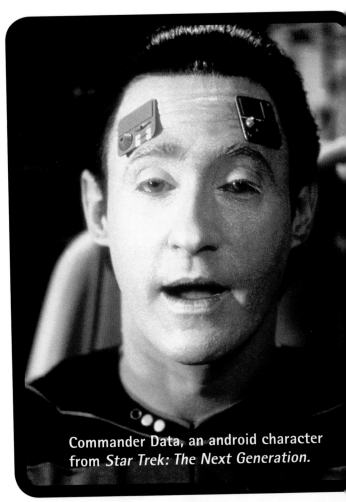

Commander Data, an android character from *Star Trek: The Next Generation*.

Up Close

ROBOT
Optimus Prime

JOB
Leader of the Autobot Transformers

SKILLS
Transforming from a giant truck into a robot

EXTRA SECTIONS
Combat Deck, Roller

SERIES
Transformers, Battlestars: Return of Convoy, Beast Wars, and *Transformers: Robots in Disguise*

Optimus Prime is the leader of the Transformers. While he is a fierce enemy of evil, he is always a good and kind leader. He uses his abilities as an inventor and mechanic to help his fellow Transformers.

Optimus Prime can separate himself into three sections. The truck's cab transforms into a robot, armed with a powerful rifle that shoots laser beams. The trailer transforms into two parts. They are the Combat Deck, a mobile battle-station, and the Roller, a small scout buggy, or four-wheel-drive vehicle.

The *Transformers* series changed often over the years, and Optimus Prime's appearance and abilities also changed. But his mighty strength and his good nature were always the same.

Cartoon robots

Japanese comics and cartoons feature many large and powerful robots. They fight in endless battles against evil invaders from other worlds.

Manga comics

During the 1950s, Japanese comic artists developed a distinctive style of artwork, called manga. Characters were drawn with large, round eyes and small features. Osamu Tezuka, an important manga artist, drew Astro Boy, as well as many other characters.

Anime

After a while the manga stories were turned into TV and movie cartoons known as anime. Anime robots are usually huge, powerful machines, loaded with weapons.

The largest machines are the mecha: huge, two-legged battle robots operated by a pilot. In the *Mobile Suit Gundam* series, smaller robotic machines are controlled by a person inside.

Mobile Suit Gundam features large robots known as mecha.

ROBOFACT

THE FIRST MECHA

The earliest mecha of the anime cartoons was Gigantor. The anime he starred in was also called *Gigantor*. It was produced during the 1960s by the team who made *Astro Boy*.

New anime

New anime science fiction series continue to appear:

※ *Full Metal Panic* features a group of teenagers. They drive giant battle mecha in their fight against evil.

※ *RahXephon* is about a teenager who controls a giant robot known as the RahXephon. Strangely, this creature is not mechanical, but is made of clay. It is also called a *dolem*, taking the name from the ancient legends of the golem.

Not all anime are science fiction stories. The anime style, with its bright colors and simple lines, is used in many Japanese cartoons. Comedy, drama, and even horror anime series are also popular.

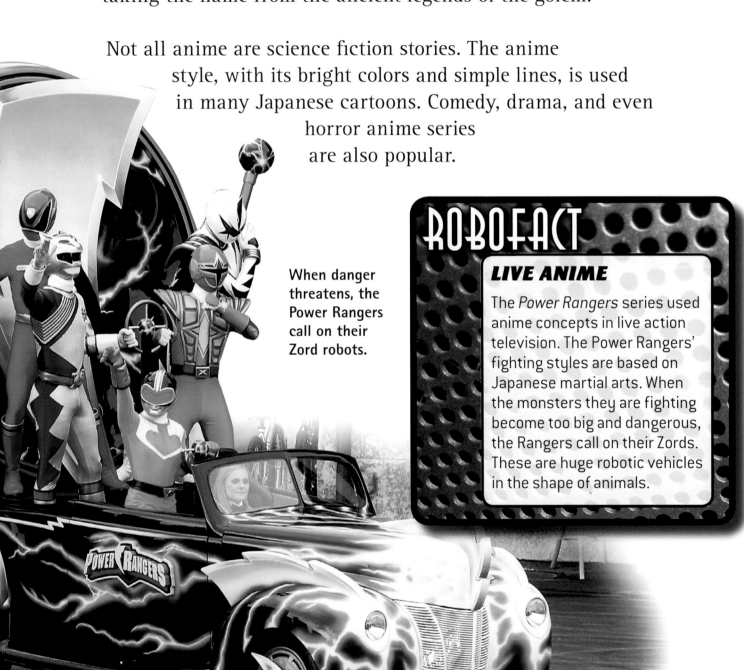

When danger threatens, the Power Rangers call on their Zord robots.

ROBOFACT

LIVE ANIME

The *Power Rangers* series used anime concepts in live action television. The Power Rangers' fighting styles are based on Japanese martial arts. When the monsters they are fighting become too big and dangerous, the Rangers call on their Zords. These are huge robotic vehicles in the shape of animals.

Toy robots

Toy companies soon realized that children wanted toys like the robots that they saw on the TV cartoons. The early toy robots could do little but move their arms and legs. Today, there are many robot toys.

The Transformers

The Transformers appeared in 1984, based on the Japanese anime style. They were toy robots, led by the powerful Optimus Prime. They could "transform" in a few moments into cars, trucks, or planes. Later, new sets of robots were designed. These new transformers could change into animals.

Optimus Prime, leader of the Transformers.

A *Transformers* cartoon movie appeared in 1989. A new *Transformers* live action movie is scheduled for release in 2007. It features human actors and computer generated images.

ROBOFACT

WHO INVENTED THE TRANSFORMERS?

The Transformers are produced by a Japanese company. However, most of the characters and stories were developed by a team of U.S. writers. These writers were experienced in writing comics.

Lego

Lego, the Danish toy company, has produced many kits that can be used for making robots. They launched the Mindstorms and NXT kits. These include a computer chip in a large plastic brick. Users load the robot's program into this chip. The kits allow users to build working robots from Lego Technic pieces such as gears, axles, and beams.

Bionicle robots

Lego also produced the Bionicle robots, a series of robotic figures that can be built and altered by their owners. Like the Transformers, the Bionicle series comes with a whole background story. They have a wide range of characters, both good and bad.

Lego's Bionicle series features many kinds of robotic creatures.

Several Bionicle movies introduce the characters and tell the story of how they have developed. The stories and the names are loosely based on Polynesian legends—stories about heroes from long ago.

Make your own robot movie

You don't need to be George Lucas or Steven Spielberg to make a movie about robots. You can make a **stop-motion animation** movie using a digital video camera, toy robots, and some **props**. You just need time and a lot of patience.

What you need

- a digital video camera
- a tripod
- lights
- toy robots
- props to fit your story

What to do

1. Make up a story to tell with your movie.
2. Mount your camera on a tripod to keep it absolutely still.
3. Put your robot characters in position in front of the camera.
4. Take a series of shots, moving the robot characters a very short distance after each shot.
5. Upload your movie to a computer and edit it using video editing software such as PowerDirector or Ulead.
5. Add a title. You might even like to add sound effects.
6. Show your movie to your friends.

If you want to make a longer movie, you will need a film crew. Friends and classmates would love to help. Don't forget to put all of their names in the credits.

Have fun!

Glossary

animators - artists who draw the characters and scenery for cartoons

artificial intelligence - the ability of a computer to think and learn like a human

astromech - a robot that works as a mechanic on space ships

computer graphics - visual artwork that is created by using computers

computer interface - a tool that allows people to communicate with computers

conflict - to clash or disagree with someone or something

director - the person in charge of making a movie or TV show

disarm - to make an unexploded bomb safe

film crew - the team of people who work on the set of a movie

gears - wheels, with teeth around the outside edges, that turn a chain or another gear

golem - a clay figure that is brought to life by a magic word

humanoid - similar in shape to a human

laser - a powerful beam of light

program - to install the instructions that control a robot's actions

props - the objects used by actors in a movie

psychologist - an expert in the workings of the human mind

pulleys - grooved wheels that ropes can run over

rabbi - a respected Jewish teacher and leader

radio-controlled models - model robots controlled by radio signals

revolt - a rebellion against authority

science fiction - stories based on futuristic scientific ideas

special effects - special techniques, such as computer graphics, used to create images that do not exist in real life

stop-motion animation - a type of animation in which objects are moved very slightly between each camera shot

surgical robots - robots capable of performing surgical operations

wire-frame outlines - three-dimensional outlines of objects, shown on a computer screen

Index